D0569342

Astrocats

Julia Harris

hamlyn

In memory of 'catman' Sam – and for
our two Samanthas

First published in Great Britain
in 2003 by
Hamlyn, a division of Octopus
Publishing Group Ltd
2–4 Heron Quays, London E14 4JP

ISBN 0 600 60766 6

A CIP catalogue record for this book
is available from the British Library

Printed and bound in China

10 9 8 7 6 5 4 3 2 1

Astrocats also appears as a regular
column in the UK's biggest-selling cat
magazine *Your Cat*.

CONTENTS

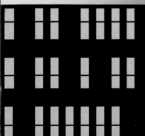

Introduction

What is it that attracts us to cats? Maybe it's their mixture of cosy domesticity, unfathomable wildness and mystery. On the one hand, they seem to embody the feminine and intuitive side of our nature, but on the other, when hunting, they display all the masculine power of the lion. Usually they are gentle and playful with humans and, unlike dogs, they don't need taking for walks every day – so they make ideal pets.

Astrology can help us to understand these complex creatures who often arrive in our homes vulnerable and bewildered. Just think, they are usually taken away from their mothers long before they would leave them in the wild, brought to live with an alien species – humans – and may never see their families again. On top of that, they are often neutered and left with no other cats for company. What a lot for one baby animal to cope with!

Cats have come in for mixed treatment through the ages, from being worshipped by the ancient Egyptians to being persecuted in medieval Europe and they have been linked to writers throughout history. Samuel Johnson, the lexicographer, had his beloved cat Hodge, who was spoiled rotten on oysters, while Raymond Chandler, the crime writer, was kept in line by Taki, his black Persian cat, whom he referred to as 'his secretary' because she seemed to monitor his writing. Female cat lovers included Colette, Stevie Smith and Beatrix Potter.

Even if you are not sure that you believe in astrology, nature has its own varying pattern from spring to winter, so it isn't surprising that cats born at different times of the year have different temperaments. Many people point out that two cats born in a litter (both the same sign) have very different temperaments, but if a natal chart was drawn up for each cat, you might find there was a different sign on the ascendant, which would change their outward character. Because we don't speak the same language as cats, often we don't know how to please them. This book should help you to understand your pet a little better. And if you are unsure of the sign your cat was born under, there is a quiz on pages 6–9 that will allow you to work out his sign. So enjoy a journey of discovery to bring you closer to your cat.

What star sign is your cat?

If you acquire a kitten that is eight to twelve weeks old, you can count back to work out his star sign. But if you don't know when your cat or kitten was born, here's a quick and easy quiz to find out what sign he was born under. If you answer 'yes' to three or more of the questions in any one section, go to the relevant questions on pages 8–9. If you don't have a majority of 'yes' answers, or you have equal amounts in several sections, try to think of his essential and 'core' character – the real him. Is this core, elemental character:

★ excitable, impulsive, brave, fiery? Go to FIRE.
★ basic, plodding, tenacious, earthy? Go to EARTH.
★ changeable, speedy, intelligent, airy? Go to AIR.
★ elusive, sensitive, deep, watery? Go to WATER.

1 Is your cat slim, nervy, energetic and intelligent?
2 Does your cat need a lot of amusing and is he never still?
3 Is he curious and does he enjoy watching TV or looking out of the window?
4 Is he sociable and does he change his mind and appear fickle?

Go to AIR.

1 Is your cat sensitive, subtle and intuitive and does he appear and disappear mysteriously?
2 Is he family-oriented, psychic (he sees things you can't) and devoted?
3 Does he form deep emotional attachments?
4 Is he devious and secretive?

Go to WATER.

1 Is your cat cautious, slow, a creature of habit and unswerving?
2 Does he get upset if his routine is altered and hate sudden change?
3 Can you set your watch by him?
4 Is he down to earth and does he work things out and plan in advance?

Go to EARTH.

1 Does your cat have mad moments and fly round the house at top speed?
2 Is he excitable, impetuous and good-natured?
3 Is he independent, a strong character and dominant?
4 Is he fearless, adaptable, fast-moving and a good hunter?

Go to FIRE.

FIRE

1 Is your cat a tearaway, difficult to train, with bad habits and a loud miaow? Does he want everything his way and right away?
Your cat is an Aries.

2 Is he lordly, big, tawny and lazy? Does he love warmth, and expect and take the best?
Your cat is a Leo.

3 Does your cat wander off? Is he clumsy, rangy, long-limbed and freedom-loving, with a cheerful look and good nature?
Your cat is a Sagittarius.

EARTH

1 Is your cat possessive, territorial, obstinate and loving? Does he form deep attachments?
Your cat is a Taurus.

2 Is he fussy over food, clean and neat, timid and yet sociable? Does he worry and like you to be punctual?
Your cat is a Virgo.

3 Does he look mournful and elegant, with good bone structure? Does he climb a lot and eat up all the scraps?
Your cat is a Capricorn.

AIR

1 Is your cat moody, changeable, a livewire with a split personality? Is he intelligent and never still?
Your cat is a Gemini.

2 Is he refined, intelligent, but lives on his nerves? Is he even-featured and very discerning?
Your cat is a Libra.

3 Is your cat an oddball who appears remote, is often away in the neighbourhood and is friendly to every other living being, including mice and spiders?
Your cat is an Aquarius.

WATER

1 Does your cat like water? Is he playful, accident-prone and untidy, and does he have trouble with his paws?
Your cat is a Pisces.

2 Has he got a delicate stomach and is he often sick? Is he very sensitive and psychic (he knows before you do that you're taking him to the vet), with a sense of humour?
Your cat is a Cancer.

3 Is he deeply attached to you, but vengeful and intense, watching your every move? Is he very jealous, showing this by hissing at your new partner or boxing the ears of the puppy you've just brought home?
Your cat is a Scorpio.

ARIES

♈ 21 March–20 April

Key characteristics

Aries is the first sign of the zodiac, and the key phrase for your Aries cat is 'I want – now!' Like a baby, he will grab at anything or any food, so be careful what you put down. And like a young child he is impatient, he can't wait. He also has childlike enthusiasm and selfishness. His Mars factor makes him energetic and demanding. If he can't get through a door, he'll yowl and scratch at it until it's opened. He is fiery, loving and playful. This cat is usually a great hunter and a Casanova. He has charisma and an endearingly eccentric streak.

A tiny tiger

You've brought your little Aries kitten home and there he is, sitting on your kitchen mat, looking bright-eyed and innocent, his ginger fur (Aries often have reddish fur) glinting in the sun. You won't realize at this point the devastation your cat will cause to feline female hearts, your home and your neighbours' gardens.

You will have years of wilful behaviour ahead of you, most of which you will forgive because this cat is such a lovable rogue.

Symbol: The Ram

Element: Fire

Aries rules: Kittens (babies), beginnings, appearance, early life from birth

Lucky colour: Red – perfect for a cat bed or cushion

Ruling planet: Mars – the energy-giver, initiator and aggressor

Compatible with: Aries, Leo, Virgo, Libra, Sagittarius and sometimes Aquarius

Fairly compatible with: Gemini, Cancer and Capricorn

Not usually compatible with: Taurus, Scorpio and Pisces

Likes:
Open doors, to be top cat, freedom, action – even if it is conflict, masses of affection, to be indulged, playing, everything instantly

Dislikes:
Being told not to do something, restraints, competition, waiting

Most kittens are like surrogate babies – they're cuddly, small and childlike and demand lots of attention – but the Aries kitten, being the first sign of the zodiac, is the most childlike creature of all. He usually has a loud miaow and rushes into danger like any two- or three-year-old child. In fact, he is very demanding all his life.

Battered ram
Aries rules the head, and many of these cats get head wounds because as kittens they hurtle into brick walls or fearlessly challenge cats and dogs six times their size. They

have little sense of danger, so need to be watched over – especially when they are young kittens. Heat and flames attract them like a magnet too, and they are likely to sizzle their whiskers and ears on lighters, stoves and log fires. The archetypal roving ginger tom is born under this sign and you will secretly admire his wicked escapades, while feigning sympathy as you listen to your neighbours' complaints about him. This is a cat who will strike fear into the hearts of all the local toms, raid next door's kitchen and shamelessly drag his booty through your cat flap. The Aries feline will adore you, but he'll demand endless affection in return, which, if he doesn't get it, could result in vengefully ripped sofas, shredded new sweaters and playful nips out of your arm.

Mad, bad and dangerous to own

He goes through his life getting his own way and doing what he wants to do, however much you try to discipline him. Only rarely will he come when he is called. When he does, you may wish you hadn't shouted, 'Tigger, come here.' You'll hear in the distance a sudden clatter of dustbin lids, which will set all the dogs in the neighbourhood

barking, then there'll be a crash of broken pottery as he knocks the wall pot down in next door's garden and a yowl of hatred as he encounters his sworn enemy, the large fearsome tabby over the fence. This caterwauling will rouse anyone in the road who isn't already wide awake.

But he'll come through the cat flap and look at you with such an innocent, loving look, you'll forgive him everything. You'll even kid yourself that he didn't really cause that commotion outside. You are just so pleased that your Aries cat is home.

The ideal owner

Although **Virgo** owners are neat and meticulous, there is something about the untamable Aries that complements their careful existence. Virgos will want to nurture and calm this impetuous cat. **Libra** is another ideal owner, as they are happy to indulge Aries and allow him to set the pace as well as look after him. A fellow **Aries** is also a good match, as long as both cat and owner have the same ideas. Nurturing **Cancer** and lively **Leo** and **Sagittarius** will also get on with an Aries, but this cat shouldn't have a **Taurus** owner – neither will give way – or a **Pisces**, who will end up with an even more chaotic home, and definitely not a **Scorpio** – these are chalk and cheese. Scorpio will be irritated by the childlike Aries, while Aries will hate Scorpio's subtle approach.

Tamed by age

As the Aries cat ages he tends to mellow, you'll be pleased to hear, and his radius of damage will be greatly reduced. Like an old cowboy who is set in his ways, he'll still do exactly as he likes (and he'll have acquired tatty ears and a broken tail along the way), but he'll sleep a lot longer, and when he's dozing he's harmless. He's the cat you love to hate, but you'd miss him more than you could imagine if he ever rode off into the sunset.

Only cat?

The attention-seeking Aries is happy to be the only cat.

He also quite enjoys being left alone for short periods. But he doesn't mind sharing with another pet as long as he is undeniably the boss.

Food for health

The Aries cat burns up so much energy that he needs plenty of red meat in his diet. A little raw mince occasionally, as part of his balanced diet, will give him added vitality too, while greens such as celery and watercress will cleanse his system. These can be chopped up finely and put in the gravy with his meat or bought in tablets formulated for cats.

Leaving your Aries cat

So long as he is well fed and looked after, this cat will quite enjoy a cattery, or someone coming into his home to feed him. But he will try to make you feel guilty about leaving him, like a child going to school for the first time. He'll wail inconsolably all the way to the cattery, then, as soon as you are out of sight, your holiday ruined by worry and guilt, he'll tuck into a big meal and pick a fight with the cat in the next cage.

TAURUS

♉ 21 April–21 May

Key characteristics

The Taurus cat has the key phrase 'I have.' Taurus cats are slow, possessive, patient and kind. But they can be very stubborn. They love their food and tend to be greedy. Because of this they can be overweight and you need to be careful about their diet. They are fixed in their ideas and, although slow to anger, when goaded they have a terrible temper, although this is very rare. Unless tormented, they are very devoted to their owners. They usually make amazing hunters, being tenacious and strong, with a great sense of timing.

Cat and bull story

Because of the mating times of cats, a great many felines are born under this sign. It's ironic, then, that there's been a superstition in the past that the May cat is unlucky. Briefly, this stems from the Celts, who misinterpreted the Druidic belief that May was a time of death and renewal. But the truth is that this is a month of great power and fertility.

Creature of habit

Taurus is easy to house-train, strong and very pretty, with a reassuringly hearty appetite. He's also wonderfully

Symbol: The Bull

Element: Earth

Taurus rules: Money, love, romance, the throat, nature, hazel trees, apple trees

Lucky colours: blue, green and pink – perfect for a radiator hammock

Ruling planet: Venus – bringer of love, harmony, food and money

Compatible with: Taurus, Cancer, Virgo, Scorpio and Pisces

Fairly compatible with: Libra, Sagittarius and Capricorn

Not usually compatible with: Aries, Gemini, Leo and Aquarius

Likes

Comfortable beds, cushions, an old-fashioned garden, love, cuddles

Dislikes

Change, the postman, cold weather, other cats in the garden, your holidays, builders

affectionate and gentle, and once he is trained he doesn't misbehave. When contented, he is reminiscent of the purring-on-the-hearthrug cat that is depicted so frequently.

In looks he often resembles a bull, with a thick, short neck, a deep, solid body and a bovine expression.

This cat is a creature of habit and loathes any disruption to his cherished routine, such as you going away for a weekend, visits to the vet, too many strangers in the house or holidays where he is left at home or taken to a cattery.

Wake-up call

He loves his creature comforts, so will appreciate a radiator hammock in the winter, the most comfortable armchair during the day and, of course, your bed to sleep on at night. The snag here is that although he will probably sleep through the night, most nights, you can expect to be woken very early to get his breakfast when he wants it. He has many ways to make sure you get up when he decides, from sitting on you (oh, what a weight!) to pawing your face, with just a fraction of claw out, so that you know he really does mean business.

He likes to have his feeding bowl and bed kept to the areas you put them in when he first arrived. The same goes for when you are training him. Never move the litter tray around or change the type of litter, unless you want trouble.

Bullish from the start

From day one he will be obstinate, and this will never change. He is also very, very strong and if you try to push him out through the cat flap when there's a sharp frost, he'll suddenly dig his paws in and, like a mule, refuse to budge. Sometimes he'll let out such a wail of annoyance, your neighbours will think you're doing something terrible to him. The Taurus cat has a huge appetite, but don't let him bully you into giving him too much. He's the sort that will approach every member of the family for food when they get up in the morning, and he'll be so insistent and so convincing that each one will think he hasn't been fed and he'll end up having seven or eight breakfasts.

Postman beware!

He is very territorial and if you think that cats don't growl, just listen to a Taurus cat when someone he doesn't like the look of comes to the door. Tales of feline attacks on postmen usually omit that the cats in question are born under this sign.

He's also a great hunter, having patience and strength. It'll come as no surprise, then, that the greatest mousers are born under the Bull. However, he does have a timid side too, and sometimes, after hissing and spitting at something or someone he doesn't like, he'll turn tail and run for his life.

When your Taurus is content he's the serenest

The ideal owner

As this cat hates to be hurried, a laid-back owner like a
Cancer, **Pisces** or another **Taurus** is ideal. A **Libra** will
appreciate this cat's looks and groom and pamper him,
Virgo enjoys a set routine like **Taurus**, while **Scorpio** will
read his soul and give him everything he wants, including
some of his roast dinner. But **Leo** would be too dominant,
Gemini would drive the Taurus cat mad with their
unpredictable mood swings; **Aries** are too impatient and
Aquarius owners' behaviour would be so alien to Taurus
that they would seem to come from a different planet.

of creatures, and this treasure of a cat rarely gets ill. He's a real comfort and will weave his way so gently into all your family's hearts that you'll never realize quite how much you love him until his solid presence is no longer there. He's part of the furniture in the nicest possible way.

Only cat?

The Taurus cat will tolerate other cats and get very fond of them if he takes a shine to them, but he doesn't like to be bossed around by another cat or dog and will either love or hate fellow pets. Give him time to adjust. Never give another pet more attention. Taurus likes to feel he is that bit special, so present him with a little treat, like catnip drops, but make sure that your other pets aren't around.

Food for health

Plenty of meaty food – beef, venison or pork. Taurus cats love milk, cream and butter, but many cats are lactose intolerant so only give him dairy products if he is used to consuming them

without side effects. Sprinkle powdered parsley in his food to keep his kidneys healthy.

Leaving your Taurus cat

He will hate catteries, so the best thing would be for you to arrange for someone to come and feed him in your home at the times he is used to. Wear something close to your skin for a few days, such as a small flannel, before you go on holiday and leave it with your Taurus when you go away. Cats have a very keen sense of smell and this will comfort him.

GEMINI

♊ 22 May–22 June

Key characteristics

Gemini is a difficult cat to understand at times, and the key phrase to his character is 'I think.' He veers from being lively, curious, sweet, adaptable, entertaining and brilliantly bright, to moody, catty, bad-tempered, spiteful and thieving. One day he'll be jealous if you pay attention to other cats or people, but the next day he won't mind. It's just that he has a dual nature. He does like to travel and explore the neighbourhood, so it's best to have an identity tag on his collar, or have him microchipped to put your mind at rest.

Double trouble

The Twins that rule this sign signify not only the desire for this cat to have a soulmate but also the duality of his nature. The Gemini cat will be a handful all his life. He is so changeable from one minute or day to the next, you could drive yourself crazy trying to work out how you have offended him. Let him get on with his moods or you could end up prematurely grey. In his own way he is completely devoted to you and you would have to go far to find a cat that is as canny and intelligent. He can't help being moody and can't explain to you why one day the world looks an

Symbol: The Twins

Element: Air

Gemini rules: Media, speed, front legs, nervous system, duality, deceit, changeability, the mind, communication

Lucky colour: Yellow – ideal for his travel blanket

Ruling planet: Mercury – the winged messenger and communicator

Compatible with: Libra, Sagittarius and Aquarius

Fairly compatible with: Aries, Gemini, Leo, Virgo and Capricorn

Not usually compatible with: Taurus, Cancer, Scorpio and Pisces

Likes

Variety, being entertained, a playmate, the latest cat gadgets, adventures, plenty of comings and going in the household, television, children

Dislikes

Being shut in, left on his own, the same cat food every day, routine, no other cats around, never being able to travel anywhere

interesting, happy place and the next even his favourite catnip mouse is boring and depressing. On a good day the world is his adventure playground, and the expression 'curiosity killed the cat' was penned for this sign. Don't worry too much, though, as he is quite streetwise; but do buy him a reflective collar, and if you live near a busy road, keep him entertained with plenty of toys at home.

A cat to confound you

These cats love a playmate, and if you don't supply another cat for them to have fun with, they might just go out and bring back a stray. And guess what? This other cat/kitten will probably look just like them, in colour and size. All Geminis will desperately seek a soulmate, and because of the need for similarity, that usually means another cat, not a human, although you will still have a big place in your pet's heart.

In fact, one day, when you think he doesn't care for you and you aren't that compatible at all, you might just find him waiting out in the rain for you, when all you've done is pop next door for a chat with your neighbour.

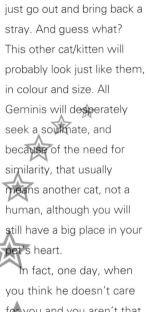

On the whole, these cats are quite self-possessed and would make ideal media cats, advertising pet food on television. Like Leos, they love the limelight.

Cat burglars

Gemini cats are never still when they are awake – you'll always see them racing around. It may even be possible to train them to wear a cat harness and go out for walks with you, provided that you live in a quiet area. Gemini cats have plenty of energy and so burn off lots of calories. However much you feed them, it's rare to see a

Gemini cat with flab, whatever their age. Being ruled by tricky Mercury, the Gemini doesn't always have strong moral scruples. When you read about felines who steal and bring things home through the cat flap, the chances are they are born under The Twins. They do appropriate objects, like the Aries cat, and you may end up with a red face when you try to explain to an irate neighbour why his new pair of socks is now in your front room … not looking quite so new.

A feline Einstein

The real plus side to your Gemini cat is that he will always look and act young – probably his lively intellect keeps him that way. When other owners tell you about the troubles they have trying to teach their cats to go out of the cat flap and not scratch the furniture, you'll be able to say, 'But my cat learned that in just a few hours.'

Your pet may not be the traditional sit-by-the-fire cat, but who wants that when you have a feline Einstein to keep you company?

Only cat?

Gemini needs a soulmate, and I'm afraid it usually isn't you. He will be

The ideal owner

Lively Gemini cats will get on well with **Libra**, who will be on the same wavelength, and **Sagittarius** owners, who respect their need for stimulation and entertainment. A Sagittarius will appreciate Gemini's adventurous streak. **Aquarius** will also admire the Gemini cat's liveliness and intelligence, while **Aries** and **Virgo** owners will think the Gemini very attractive and will probably hold conversations with him. **Taurus** and **Cancer** would find the Gemini too frisky – these owners like peace and quiet, while the **Scorpio** owner would think the Gemini cat two-faced and the sensitive **Pisces** would be upset by the Gemini cat's lack of emotion.

happiest with another cat
similar in looks and age to
himself. He does tend to
wander and will probably
try to follow you down the
road when you go out, but
another cat companion
might curtail his curiosity a

bit. Even when the Gemini
cat has a companion, he
might suddenly ignore
them or pick a fight out of
the blue. You just can't
gauge his behaviour,
because of his dual nature,
but on the whole he still

prefers to have company rather than be alone.

Food for health

These cats need plenty of B vitamins to feed their nerves, as they can become worried and irritable, so give them brewer's yeast tablets to keep them fit. Brewer's yeast will also help to keep the fleas away and give them a good shiny coat. Small amounts of fish oil or vitamin E oil, perhaps fed to them once a week, will keep their fur and skin in good condition too, as often their nerves make them break out in skin irritations.

Leaving your Gemini cat

This cat will enjoy holidays, whether it's a stay at a cattery or coming with you. The Gemini cat travels well and adapts to unusual surroundings, finding it a big adventure. He'll love to sleep in his cat carrier, even when he's at home. He may even enjoy staying at home if interesting people come round to feed him. A home-sitter would suit him too, although once he realizes he has round-the-clock care, he could spend a lot of time out in his usual style.

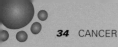

CANCER

♋ 23 June–23 July

Key characteristics

The Cancer cat has the key phrase 'I nurture'. He's caring and intuits his way through life. A creature who pussyfoots around everything and senses the atmosphere, he is rarely direct. Subtle, sensitive, moody and gentle, he has a delicate digestion. Often he suffers from upset stomachs, fears and phobias. This feline is mysterious, psychic and family-oriented, and he has a sixth sense about what will happen in the family. He can be a bit of a hypochondriac.

Your psychic pet

Out of all the signs, Cancer is the most stereotypically cat-like. For these are truly creatures of the moon and the night. In olden times, Cancer ruled the sea and travelling and this was the sign of the wanderer. Even today, although Cancer has come to embody the hearth and home more, this sign still likes moving house, and you could find your Moon-ruled cat surprisingly adaptable should you have to uproot and live in another area, because his greatest attachment is to you and your family. In fact, to him, he is just another member of that family, full stop.

Symbol: The Crab

Element: Water

Cancer rules: Sailors, the sea, travel, the home and family, food and catering, nurturing

Lucky colour: Silver – a reflective collar keeps him safe

Ruling planet: The Moon – moody, emotional, nurturing and changeable

Compatible with: Taurus, Leo, Scorpio and Pisces

Fairly compatible with: Aries, Cancer, Libra, Sagittarius and Capricorn

Not usually compatible with: Gemini, Virgo and Aquarius

Likes

The family to be at home with him, plenty of food, the kitchen, everyone being happy, being petted

Dislikes

You leaving the house, discord, any family member being away for too long

These sensitive creatures have particularly mysterious eyes, which are usually large and round. Like the Pisces cat, Cancer is very psychic. You might see your cat staring intently at something in space although there is nothing there. Or he could play with a seemingly imaginary cat and rush up as if to meet someone who is not visible to you.

Everything about this feline is sensuous and subtle, and just like the crab, their symbol, they won't approach anything directly. If they are hungry, most cats will swish around you with their tails and miaow, making it obvious that food in on their mind. But the Cancer cat could give you a silent miaow. This is his way of saying, 'I am so faint and weak with hunger and so starved (even though I had a big breakfast this morning) that I can hardly raise the strength to ask for food.'

Crab that cares

Cancer cats have an offbeat sense of humour, which will delight the whole household. A favourite game is to play hide-and-seek with you and pounce out at you from under the bed.

When caring for your Cancer cat, remember how delicate he is physically. He is particularly sensitive to chemicals and it would be best to treat him with natural, gentle preparations for fleas and parasites if possible. But you'll never have to worry about this cat being bad-tempered with your children or other family members. He'll sleep on the beds with your kids when they are ill to comfort them, and will seem to know when you are happy or sad and empathize in a very caring way. He will also sense when you are about to take him to the vet and will disappear, even though you have been very careful not to give him any clues. And before you go on holiday he'll become sad and morose, although there isn't a suitcase in sight.

Cancers are very moody cats altogether and periodically they get upset. It could be the weather, the food you gave them, biorhythms, a sudden new phobia or next door's cat – you'll probably never know. These crabby moments can sometimes make them unapproachable, but although they may hiss when having a bad day, they are rarely aggressive and they'll soon be their sunny selves again.

Puss in boats

In days gone by, when sailors often had a ship's cat, the Cancer feline would have been ideal, as this sign rules sea travel. Cancer rules kith and kin too, so there would have been a family atmosphere on the boat as well.

Nowadays this cat will make the best ever pet, and if you remember to treat him sensitively, like one of your family, the love, companionship and care he gives you in return will be more than you could ever have hoped for.

The ideal owner

Scorpio and **Taurus** have the same home-loving instincts as the Cancer cat, and they will ensure that he is deeply loved and has plenty of good food. Also, both these signs take things at a slow and measured pace, which is comforting for the Cancer cat. **Capricorn** would also be suitable and has the same traditional outlook as the Moon-ruled cat, looking back on the past as this sign does. **Pisces** would be compatible too, sharing the same dreaminess. These two would probably communicate by telepathy, while **Leo** would defend the sensitive Crab. **Geminis** would be too lively for the Cancer cat, **Virgos** too uptight and frugal, and the **Aquarius** owner wouldn't understand the subtle moods or Cancer's need for a close, loving family.

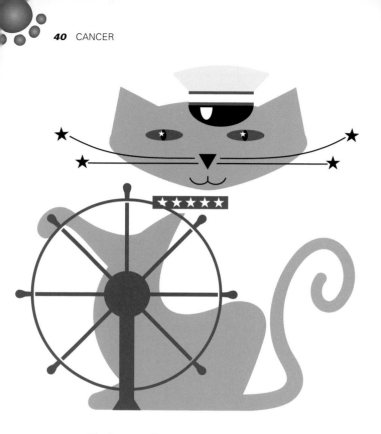

Only cat?

Cancer cats are so devoted to you and your family, they'll be quite happy being the only cats, but if you introduce other felines, their caring natures will let them take them to their hearts.

Be careful, though, not to bring home a bossy cat or dog, or your pet could feel insecure. A Pisces or Scorpio would be ideal.

Food for health

Cancers have very delicate stomachs, so little and often is best for them. Avoid giving them too much food or overly rich meals. They are usually fond of fish, with gently poached cod or haddock being a special treat for them. If they have upset stomachs, a little well-cooked rice mixed in with their food will help settle them. Keep their diets to fish and white meat for a while until they are better.

Leaving your Cancer cat

Whatever you do, your holiday will be very upsetting for your devoted Cancer cat. He'll probably respond by having an upset stomach and being sick. He hates his little world being turned upside down. Even if you have cat-sitters in, he will still pine for you (but maybe this is better than putting him in a cattery). When you return from your holiday, you and your family will get the warmest welcome of your lives – it's something you will never forget.

LEO

♌ 23 July–23 August

Key characteristics

The Leo cat has the key phrase 'I create' and his main aim is to enjoy himself. He loves playing and is adventurous. He naturally rules the household and has a regal bearing. Everything has to be big with this cat, from his food portions to his favourite chair. In temperament he is kind, good-natured and brave. Although he is moody at times, he likes those around him to be happy. He basks in attention and being pampered and loves the limelight. Even if he gets ill, he makes sure he enjoys life and won't feel sorry for himself.

King of your household

If the tawny, amber-eyed lion is the king of the jungle, then your Leo pussycat is king of your household. Of course, most cats rule the house, but none quite so effortlessly as the Leo, even if he is a small, bijou feline. Is he stretched out across the hall? Then you will just step over him. Or is he lying full out across your best sofa in front of the television? Then you'll find you naturally sit on the floor, even though it may be a bit uncomfortable. You wouldn't dream of disturbing your regal Leo cat and incurring his displeasure. It would be a bit like asking royalty to move for you.

Symbol: The Lion

Element: Fire

Leo rules: Play, creativity, having fun, romance, bravery, nobleness, toys

Lucky colour: Gold – perfect for his identity disc

Ruling planet: The Sun – the life force and giver of good health

Compatible with: Aries, Cancer, Virgo, Sagittarius and sometimes Scorpio

Fairly compatible with: Gemini, Leo and Aquarius

Not usually compatible with: Taurus, Libra, Capricorn and Pisces

Mane attraction

When you first take your Leo kitten home, you'll marvel at how big he is, how strong and how playful. Of course, he is a handful, but you'll be mesmerized by his clever antics and his huge personality. This is a cat who has real presence.

He will always love warmth and sleeping in the sun. You will have to be careful and guard his nose and ears against sunburn if he is pale-coloured, as he'll stretch out on the patio from dawn to dusk in the summer. After all this cat's ruling planet is the Sun!

Likes

Warmth, rest, play, being the centre of attention,everything on a grand scale, his own way in everything

Dislikes

Being ignored, meagreness, small portions, cramped conditions, coldness

There is always a tawny look about a Leo. Even if he is black and white, he will probably have golden eyes and a thick ruff of fur around his neck, like a mane. He is a very amorous cat and will have a lot of adoring female felines as well as human admirers.

No one plays as hard as a Leo cat and no other cat can sleep for such long periods. He doesn't do anything by halves. He needs loads of attention and will become upset if he is ignored or not in the limelight. When you have guests, he will take centre stage, basking in all the admiring comments he gets. He's a cat who adores being adored. He tends to be dramatic in everything he does and his ideal habitat, apart from pride of place in your home, would be as a theatre cat, where he could stroll on stage every now and then. Theatre cats are always petted and pampered.

Catty lionesses

Unlike the males, female Leos can be quick-tempered, especially with other cats, and they can get very jealous if you give too much attention to another feline. If they were human, you would describe them as catty.

Most Leos have a sunny disposition, and their enormous personalities will make them loved by all. Perhaps more than any other sign they will be a very difficult creature to replace, as you will think that no other cat has quite such a tremendous character.

Only cat?

Leo is happy to be the only cat, but if there are other felines or dogs, he will naturally be top of the pecking order, so there shouldn't be a problem. All the animals in the house, plus humans, will realize they are inferior to this mighty being and without questioning will give him the run of the household. Any cheekiness from another cat or dog and he will soon put them in their place with a swift bat of his paw. The culprit will not reoffend.

Food for health

Leo rules the back and heart, so he needs food that will keep his heart and his bones healthy. Avoid anything too fatty, although some fat is vital for cats. Also, try to avoid processed foods (as long as your cat has a balanced diet) and make sure he has some greens, even if they

The ideal owner

A Leo needs to be waited on and pampered, so a very good owner is the **Virgo**, who will love to serve him. The only snag is that Leos like large portions of food and Virgos tend to be frugal. Nevertheless, the Virgo will adore this cat and give him everything he wants. **Aries** is another good owner, because he has the same playful nature as Leo. Once hooked on his Leo feline, the Aries will move heaven and earth to give his cat what he wants. **Sagittarius** shares this cat's love of adventure, while **Cancer** nurtures him and **Scorpio** owners admire his strength. With **Taurus** there would be a battle of wills and **Libra** would be too sensitive. **Pisces** would find this cat too demanding and **Capricorn** would think him attention-seeking.

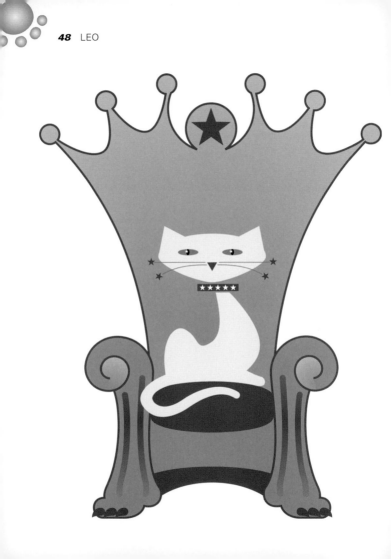

are mashed up with the meat. To strengthen his bones and back, give him calcium-rich marrow from within the bones and gristly meat. Also supplement his diet with some cat vitamin tablets that are calcium-enriched.

Leaving your Leo cat

As long as you take your Leo to a five-star cattery with television, heated beds and plenty of space, you needn't worry too much about him. And if he's comfortable and waited on, he'll look on the episode as an adventure, but he will be glad to get home. He does like to have a lot of space to reign over. This is a cat who would love to travel abroad with you, so get his passport ready. And he'll be especially happy if you go somewhere luxururious and warm. He'll enjoy travelling and will bask in the sun at your tropical resort and make himself at home very quickly. As long as he has the same luxuries he enjoys at home – like the best food and sleeping quarters – there'll be no complaints from him.

VIRGO

♍ 24 August–23 September

Key characteristics

The Virgo cat has the key phrase 'I serve.' Virgos are patient and caring. This cat will soothe you if you are ill, is neat and clean, but is fussy with food. Like Capricorns, he likes order, tidiness and routine. Because he lacks confidence, he needs plenty of reassurance, praise and encouragement. He isn't overtly affectionate, but likes you to make a fuss of him. He can become bad-tempered and hiss under stress, and is of a nervous disposition. He is a terrible worrier. Virgos like to be amused and entertained, otherwise they can get bored.

Neat and sweet

In most ways your Virgo cat is a pleasure to be with. And with the right owner the devotion will be mutual, lasting a lifetime. There will be no mess when he's a kitten. He'll take to the kitty litter like a duck to water because he was born a neat cat. Furthermore, he's gentle and careful, so your ornaments should stay intact. As long as you are a fastidious, careful owner who lives to a regular routine, your little Virgo will always be serene and happy. But if there's any disruption, he will fret and worry.

Symbol: The Virgin

Element: Earth

Virgo rules: Nurses, service to others, small animals (like cats!), fine details, criticism, cleanliness, modesty

Lucky colour: Green – this will soothe your Virgo so give him a deep green cushion

Ruling planet: Mercury – sociable and communicative traveller

Compatible with: Aries, Taurus, Leo, Virgo and Capricorn

Fairly compatible with: Scorpio, Aquarius and Pisces

Not usually compatible with: Gemini, Cancer, Libra and Sagittarius

Likes:

Order, cleanliness, everything on time, quietness, praise and reassurance

Dislikes:

Chaos, dirt, food that isn't fresh, criticism and the unexpected

Curious and cute

Because he is ruled by Mercury, the planet of communication, he is a very sociable little creature, so whether you have other pets, or friends round, he will enjoy their company and take an interest in everything that's going on. Most cats like looking out of the window, but your Virgo cat is particularly curious and loves people-watching. If you make sure he has a wide, comfortable windowsill for this purpose, he will be kept amused for hours and hours.

In looks it appears as if his creator has taken special

care with his markings. If he is a tabby his stripes will be especially orderly, while if he is black and white his markings will look precision-painted. He usually has beautiful, big, clear eyes and an especially careful way of sitting, with his tail curled neatly around him, whether he's in front of the fire or on a chair.

Pill-popping puss

This cat is wonderfully patient. He'll wait up for you by the door, hour after hour, if you come in late. And he has a special affinity with hospitals and illness. When you are under the weather he seems to know and is particularly sympathetic and soothing, patiently sitting with you. He'll do everything he can to please you and will sleep on your bed, almost willing you to get better. But he is a bit of a hypochondriac himself, especially if he is upset by you not sticking to a regular routine.

Cats with phantom pregnancies or who have undiagnosable conditions are born under this sign. Keep a little medicine chest in his view, with bandages, homoeopathic remedies and cream for his cuts and grazes. Then he will know he'll be well looked after.

Quietly caring

This sign lacks confidence and needs lots of love and praise from his owner. Don't be put off if your Virgo doesn't rush up to you and purr when you come in after work. He isn't overly demonstrative, but that doesn't mean he doesn't care for you. He does – deeply. And just because he cleans himself every time you touch him doesn't mean he thinks you are a grubby human – this is just his ultra fastidiousness. Even if a few raindrops touch his coat he will give himself a good wash. Life with your Virgo cat should be a long and happy partnership, as he'll be the easiest of creatures to get along with, give or take a few phobias and eccentricities. He will quietly and calmly be your companion for all his days.

Food for health

This is a near-perfect cat, but there is one thing you may have trouble with and that is his food. This feline could drive you to try every available cat food there is, and just when you think that at last you've found the food he likes (probably organic – there is quite a lot of this food for cats on

The ideal owner

Taurus will give the Virgo cat all the security he needs and keep to a reassuring routine. The only difficulty with this duo is that food-obsessed Taurus will worry that Virgo isn't eating enough and will have a few sleepless nights wondering what to feed him. **Capricorn** will be an excellent owner. Both human and cat like to live simply, frugally and with structure. Another **Virgo** will also get on well with this sign as they will understand each other perfectly. A **Leo** would appreciate the **Virgo** not hogging the limelight, and an **Aries** would give them a challenge. But the Virgo cat won't get on with a happy-go-lucky **Sagittarius**, an emotional and chaotic **Cancer** owner or a **Libra**, who would not have the routine the **Virgo** needs.

the market now to
supplement the fresh food
you buy) he'll suddenly turn
up his nose at it, or just

pick. Fresh and portions
not too big really are best
for him, and he may enjoy
several small meals rather

than two medium ones
each day.

Leaving your
Virgo cat

Whatever you do with your
Virgo cat, whether you
take him to a cattery or
leave him at home, with
a neighbour calling in, he
will try his best to adapt.
But you would do well to
bear in mind that this cat is
a terrible worrier and is
also very much a creature
of habit.

If he is at a cattery and
his routine is very different,
he might get upset. And
however much you tell
the owner that your cat
never complains, damages
your property or makes a
mess, if everything is too
strange and scary for him,
they might have a different
story to tell you when
you return from your break.
They will probably report
that he did settle down in
the end – but it was
only the day before you
arrived back.

The kindest thing for
your Virgo cat is a house-
sitter, who keeps to his
routine, or a neighbour or
friend who will call in with
regular meals and care.
Then your Virgo will be the
serenest of felines while
you are away.

LIBRA

♎ 24 September–23 October

Key characteristics

Libra's key phrase is 'I balance.' This cat needs harmony, peace and, like Gemini, a soulmate. He hates loud noise, vulgarity and bad taste. He also loathes discord and people quarrelling around him. He can suffer from mental illness if he is in the wrong surroundings or he is unhappy. He is loving, beautiful, easy to live with and adaptable. He likes soft, pastel colours, attractive surroundings and to be pampered. He doesn't like anyone who is over-possessive or too emotional. He'll always look well groomed, even if he's (perish the thought) been in a fight with another cat or a dog.

A sensitive balance

Libra cats are beautiful, with even features and great refinement. They love to recline on soft cushions in exquisite surroundings and they make ideal cats for showing. A cat show gives them attention, pampering, novelty in meeting new people and praise when they win – everything that a Libra can want. These cats also look good in glossy magazine adverts. They are clean and neat. Even if you live on a farm, they'll never get their paws muddy or look unkempt. They also seem to bring an aura of calm to

Symbol: The Scales

Element: Air

Libra rules: Marriage, beauty, refinement, the law, books, perfect physical symmetry

Lucky colour: Pastel pink and pale blue – perfect for a cosy blanket

Ruling planet: Venus – bringing refinement, beauty and harmony

Compatible with: Aries, Gemini, sometimes Cancer, and Aquarius

Fairly compatible with: Taurus and Libra

Not usually compatible with: Leo, Virgo, Scorpio, Sagittarius, Capricorn and Pisces

Likes
Being groomed and pampered, peace, serenity, refinement, intelligent owners

Dislikes
Chaos, discord, quarrels, neglect in being groomed, unfairness, untidiness

any situation, managing to find a peaceful place to look beautiful in, even if your home has subsidence and the builders are excavating the house room by room. These gorgeous and refined creatures love beautiful things, so an artistic cat bed will delight them. Never give them a choice of food. They have terrible trouble making decisions and will first look at the milk, then the fish, and become really confused. They can't bear raised voices, so if you and your partner quarrel it will upset your highly strung Libra, putting him off his meals.

Libra's library

The contradictory thing about Libra cats is that, although they look so calm and manage to stay so neat, they are a bundle of nerves inside. They can be almost Cancerian in their crabbiness if there is some permanent discord in their lives. These cats can live on the edge, and felines with behavioural problems that require a visit to a cat shrink are often born under the Scales. Sometimes it's because they just can't cope with the unbearable harshness of everyday life.

Libra has an affinity with books, so don't be surprised if your Libra cat reclines on one of your bookshelves. He may not be able to read them, but he picks up the erudite vibes and finds them restful to be near. It also gives him a safe place to get away from it all.

TLC for your cat

This sensitive creature will love to be pampered. Most cats hate being bathed, brushed and combed, but your Libra will revel in all the attention and grooming. He is keen on cleanliness, so he will be very grateful if he can look his best at all times. And he will also like to have a beautiful collar, whether it is studded with stones or just a lovely coloured velvet one.

This attractive cat is very loving, but there is a fickleness about him too. Just when you think he is deeply devoted to you, he could switch his affections to another member of the family, waiting up for them and giving them all the attention he was giving you a few days ago.

Console yourself with the fact that he is never aggressive or messy and he doesn't deliberately set out to be disloyal. In fact his very fickleness could stem from trying to be fair. This cat hates injustice – it

would be very hurtful for him if you favoured and petted another of your cats or dogs more than him. And the way he shares his affections with first one member of the family and then another could be his way of making sure everyone, including your visiting distant cousin, gets their fair share of love.

Like Taurus, Libra loves the best, from velvet cushions to gourmet food. And he enjoys himself when you have guests round to dinner. Then he has someone new to admire him. Being praised and pampered will make your Libra cat happy – the

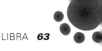

The ideal owner

Gemini and **Aquarius** share the same mental liveliness as the Libra cat, so will understand his need to be entertained and have a variety of things to do. They will also like the same minimalist, airy decor as the Libra cat. **Taurus** can also nurture Libra, as they are both ruled by Venus and love good food and beautiful things. The opposite sign, **Aries**, helps the Libra cat to be positive, instead of wavering over which food to eat and what door to go out of, as Libra is so indecisive. **Cancer** will be sensitive to the Libra's needs too, and will do their best to make gentle Libra comfortable. **Capricorn** owners would be too tough for Libra and **Leo** too dominant. Other bad matches would be critical **Virgo**, rough and ready **Sagittarius**, chaotic **Pisces** and intense **Scorpio**.

more you give him attention, the more he'll appreciate it and love you in return.

Only cat?

Libra likes to have people around him, and other pets as long as they are not disruptive. But a great big boisterous dog or a rampaging tomcat would give him an attack of nerves and he might develop all kinds of psychosomatic illnesses. Libra needs a companion as refined and gentle as himself. He gets easily bored, so he needs the

mental stimulation and companionship that other pets bring. Just as long as he has a quiet place he can retreat to in the house, he will get on with most other animals, but sometimes he finds rowdy children too much to cope with.

Food for health

Libra has a delicately balanced nervous system. Not only does he need his B vitamins, found in yeast tablets, but he also likes his meals to be nicely presented. Try cutting his meat or fish into bite size pieces and sprinkle his food with his favourite biscuits.

Leaving your Libra cat

Your well-mannered Libra will behave while you are on holiday, but if you go away he would prefer to have some company. He may get lonely just left in the house with someone calling in for meals, even if they do spend a little time with him. Perhaps a cattery would be best, as he will like to talk to the other pets and will probably enjoy his new surroundings. Usually he doesn't mind being contained for a while and will lounge around looking beautiful and decorative. But he will like to be groomed and his pen to be kept clean.

SCORPIO

♏ 24 October–22 November

Key characteristics

The Scorpio cat has the key phrase 'I control.' He is very intense and needs someone who can make him relax. He watches everything you do and then works out what you will do next. He is extremely observant but doesn't like the same scrutiny himself. He's very interested in sex and will be ultra loyal to you, but if you or anyone upset him he can be vengeful. He likes to have secrets and doesn't want you to pry into all his little hideouts. He is exceptionally resilient if he is ill and has amazing recuperative powers.

Powerful puss

When this powerhouse of energy is a kitten he will be so intense he'll wear you out. He will watch everything you do and when you brush your teeth he'll make his way up to your bed – he knows that's where you'll be going next, he's got it all worked out. Even as a kitten he seems more mature than the average cat. He puts up with visits to the vet and discipline with stoical calm. Your Scorpio feline is exceptionally loyal and devoted, but this is coupled with an almost insane jealousy of your relationships with partners, friends and other animals.

Symbol: The Scorpion

Element: Water

Scorpio rules: Sex, regeneration, secrets, investigations, birth and death

Lucky colour: Wine – perfect for his velvet collar

Ruling planet: Pluto – the grand transformer, bringing to light hidden things

Compatible with: Taurus, Cancer, sometimes Leo, and Capricorn

Fairly compatible with: Virgo, Scorpio and Pisces

Not usually compatible with: Aries, Gemini, Libra, Sagittarius and Aquarius

Likes

Cosy evenings in with just you, night time, cellars, attics, quietness, secret hiding places, hunting

Dislikes

Change, visitors who keep calling him 'kitty', next door's dog, having nowhere to hide

It's all right if he takes to whoever you bring home, but if he doesn't he has the most devious ways of showing his displeasure. He might take to his bed and pretend to be ill when a visitor he can't stand overstays their welcome, then bounce back to life the minute they go. Or he might stare at the person with such intensity they feel uncomfortable and leave. Rarely does he openly attack, but he could make his way to the hall and spray against your guest's coat or, if he's black, sleep on their white coat, so it's covered in hair. If he's white he'll pick something black to ruin.

Don't say that you haven't been warned!

Feline with stamina

When this cat is ill he has the most amazing patience and recuperative powers. He'll cling on to life at times against all odds, and even when you take him to the vet on his last journey, because you think it's the kindest thing to do, he could suddenly make a miraculous recovery just as you prepare him for his big sleep.

He has great powers of perception too. He will know when you are upset or ill, and will look at you with such penetrating and mesmerizing eyes, you'll know he understands all you are going through.

True to you, in his fashion

Although this cat is undividedly loyal to you and expects the same in return, he does have a secret life – one that you may never get to know. This is just part of being a Scorpio and you will not change him. You might have him for years before finding out that he spends the hours when you are at work with a neighbour who has been feeding fresh salmon to your beautiful, sleek and hypnotic-eyed cat. Your suspicions may first be aroused when your Scorpio turns his nose up at the haddock you've cooked him and looks a bit overweight. Later his unfaithfulness is confirmed when your neighbour openly admits he visits each afternoon. You may be hurt, but don't retaliate by inviting round a friend you know your cat hates. Scorpio cats always demand that you toe the line, but they expect you to be able to tolerate their little indiscretions.

It is you he loves, make no mistake about that, and his ability to comfort and understand you when you are troubled or ill will make you love him for ever. You will even forgive the fact that he spits at and scratches your best friend or partner when they get too much attention.

Only cat?

Although occasionally the Scorpio cat will take to another cat or dog, he is happy to be the only cat. His ability to enjoy a certain amount of solitude and make you the sole focus of his affections makes him ideal to be the only feline. But another cat or dog with a compatible sign could be introduced, with great care. However, never give the other pet more attention than your Scorpio.

The ideal owner

One of the best signs for a Scorpio cat is **Cancer**. These two have a mutual depth of understanding that is hard to match. They are sensitive to each other's feelings and the Cancer owner will tolerate any over-possessiveness. **Taurus** comes a close second to the Cancer owner. Taurus understands the jealousy of this cat, because he is possessive and sometimes insanely jealous, too. Both these signs like a traditional home and they also appreciate good food. Another good owner would be the **Capricorn**, as both signs take life seriously. **Leo**, too, would admire the Scorpio strength of will. The Scorpio cat would find a **Gemini** or **Libra** owner too lightweight for his intense, possessive nature. An **Aries** would be too extrovert, **Sagittarius** over-sporty and **Aquarius** rather impersonal.

Food for health

Scorpio cats love rich food and plenty of it. They also tend not to take enough exercise, so their owners need to be careful that they don't become obese. These felines often have trouble with their bowels, being prone to either constipation or diarrhoea, so they need food that keeps their digestion balanced.

Avoid foods that are too dry, like all biscuits, which will block them, and those that are too moist or contain too much liver or fish oil. You need to find the happy medium with their diet.

Leaving your Scorpio cat

Although he won't enjoy a cattery, this is a stoical cat and he will endure the separation from you calmly. There will be more of a problem when you return. Instead of purring a greeting, he could get his revenge by pretending that he doesn't know you until such time as he feels able to forgive you. Or he could have a few 'accidents' in the house, just to let you know you have upset him deeply. Eventually, though, you will be back in his affections.

SAGITTARIUS

↗ 23 November–21 December

Key characteristics

The Sagittarius cat has the key phrase 'I dare.' This feline is always cheerful and full of optimism. Clumsy, speedy and with long legs, he has a rangy look and loves the outdoors. He hates to feel constricted and enjoys complete freedom. This is a cat who would loathe to be confined to a city flat with no means of getting out. His nature is kind, but he can be thoughtless and tactless too. Being very independent, if he ever had to fend for himself (after getting lost, for example), he'd be a survivor.

A country cat

These cats are country animals at heart. There is something untamable about the Sagittarius feline and, sadly for you, you should lock away your ornaments for his whole lifetime. That is if you value your best vase. He never seems to understand that he should slow down or look where he is going. And added to that he is just plain clumsy too. The cat ruled by the Archer is very independent and he'd be happiest in a big farmhouse kitchen where boots are covered in mud, dogs come and go, and dirty pawprints do not attract too much attention.

Symbol: The Archer (half man, half horse)

Element: Fire

Sagittarius rules: Long-distance travel, learning, positivity, altruism

Lucky colours: Indigo, purple – perfect for his pet carrier on car journeys

Ruling planet: Jupiter – jovial, luck-bringer

Compatible with: Aries, Gemini, Leo and Aquarius

Fairly compatible with: Taurus, Cancer and Sagittarius

Not usually compatible with: Virgo, Libra, Scorpio, Capricorn and Pisces

Likes

A sense of freedom, wide open spaces, an ever-open cat flap, a happy-go-lucky owner

Dislikes

A houseproud owner, being shut in, people who are miserable, controlling or critical

Happy hunter

A Sagittarius cat loves the great outdoors and enjoys chasing his prey, whether it's a pretty female cat, a rabbit or a bird. But once the hunt is over he often loses interest – he's a humanitarian type of animal, with a sense of justice – and could catch a mouse, only to let it go unharmed, in your house. You will spend a lot of time worrying where he's got to when he disappears (which he does very frequently), but when he is home he wreaks havoc. You just can't win, but equally you can't help loving this big, untidy rogue who seems all tail and legs.

Accident-prone archer

You could spend a great many of your days going backwards and forwards to the vet as your pet first has to have his back leg in plaster and then his front paw. Next his neck has to be put in a brace. Pet insurance is a must or you will end up penniless. The vet will start getting suspicious too. Are you really taking good care of your cat? Why does he have so many mishaps all the time?

He does go off on long rambles too, sometimes for days. At first you'll put up 'missing' posters, but after the tenth time of turning up on your doorstep thin and hungry, just when you'd given up hope, you'll stop sending out the search parties and notifying the vets and the animal shelters, although you'll never stop worrying about him.

Say it with a smile

Ruled by cheerful Jupiter, this cat will be a joy when you are down. He is a real clown and a great personality. You just can't stay depressed for too long when he's around. It may be the way he looks at you with that happy expression, or it may be his latest escapade, when he ended up with sizzled whiskers after he stole a spare rib from next door's barbecue. Somehow he always manages to put a smile on your face.

This is a cat who not only knows the whole neighbourhood but also travels even further afield when he gets a chance. You will be shocked when one of your neighbours tells you that she saw your Rufus twenty miles away. 'I know it was him,' your neighbour says. 'I could tell by his tatty ear and his collar – and no other cat walks in quite the same way as he does. And anyway, he recognized me as soon as I called.'

Life to this cat is a big adventure, and that means exploring as much as possible. He does have luck on his side as his ruler Jupiter is not only joyful and expansive but also gives him nine lives (well, nine is his lucky number), so try not to worry too much when he disappears yet again.

Only cat?

Sagittarius cats don't go in for the territorial bit too much (they are out such a lot they don't have time for possessiveness), so they would be quite happy for

The ideal owner

An **Aries** would have fun playing with the lively Sagittarius. Sagittarius cats can't bear miseries or worriers, so a **Leo** owner would be right up his street. The only snag is that Leos love their possessions and don't want their fabulously expensive Chinese rugs ruined by a big, bouncing mud-covered feline. **Cancer** make good owners because, although these signs are worlds apart in many ways, Cancer will want to mother this wild cat, forgiving him his many mad moments. **Gemini** and **Aquarius** are good bets too – a Gemini owner won't notice that the Sagittarius isn't always around; and the same goes for the scatty Aquarius owner. But **Virgo** owners will be too neat, while **Libra** will be over-sensitive, **Scorpio** over-possessive, **Capricorn** rigid and **Pisces** too weak.

you to have another cat or a dog. They are very friendly, but they are very independent too, so whether they are an only cat or not, they will be equally cheerful.

Food for health

These cats have good healthy appetites and they aren't fussy eaters. Feed them plenty of calcium-rich marrow from within bones, or seaweed, spinach or broccoli, as the calcium will help in case of broken limbs.

Leaving your Sagittarius cat

These cats would like you to take them with you when you go away. They would love to travel wherever you go, but of course you would then spend the whole time worrying that they would disappear. Because of that, perhaps the best thing is to have someone call round to your home every day and leave food and water for your cat. Having a pet-sitter would be an expensive option and, since your cat is hardly ever at home, it would be an unnecessary outlay. Your Sagittarius cat won't need any comfort round a warm fire while you are away but he'll be really pleased when you return.

CAPRICORN

♑ 22 December–20 January

Key characteristics

The Capricorn cat's key phrase is 'I use.' He is a down-to-earth cat that likes routine but is also very intellectual. He looks sad but has a dry sense of humour and he is very keen on punctuality (he's a clock-watcher for his meals). This cat likes to climb up curtains and trees, is long-lived and has a youthful appearance as he gets older. As he can stagnate, he needs to be made to exercise. He'll eat almost any food and is frugal, not liking to waste anything. He is very loyal to his family, whether it is you or the cat family he came from.

Handsome old goat

This cat has all the qualities that should ensure he lives to a ripe old age. He also wears well and will look younger and younger as he gets older, with behaviour to match. To help his longevity, he doesn't go rushing into danger and he rarely wanders far away from home. He is very careful and circumspect in his behaviour, and although it is ideal for a cat to have a big garden, the Capricorn can live in a small house with just a courtyard and be quite happy.

Like the Virgo, he is a creature of habit. He wants everything to be in the right place and to have his meals on

Symbol: The Goat

Element: Earth

Capricorn rules: Time, the skeleton, bones, teeth, professions, power, old age, framework, death, restriction

Lucky colour: Brown – this colour makes the Capricorn feel secure

Ruling planet: Saturn – gives a framework to life and responsibilities

Compatible with: Virgo, Scorpio and Capricorn

Fairly compatible with: Aries, Taurus, Cancer and Aquarius

Not usually compatible with: Gemini, Leo, Libra, Sagittarius and Pisces

Likes

Routine, tidiness, a slow pace, peace and quiet, churchyards, love, reassurance, praise

Dislikes

Noise, discordant music, uncultured owners, untidy rooms, minimalism, not being praised or appreciated

time. He usually has excellent bone structure, which means he often has the look of an ancient Egyptian cat. Like a mountain goat, he loves to climb, whether it's up your legs as a kitten (ouch!) or up the curtains, so a tall activity centre would be ideal for him. He often takes a tumble when running up a tree or the stairs, but then he'll just dust himself off and start all over again.

Kitten on the keys

Usually your Capricorn cat has a very sad expression and at first you could find yourself spending a fortune on treats for him to try to cheer him up – until you eventually realize he always looks like this, even when he's happy.

When you have visitors you can count on Capricorn to have excellent manners. He will get on well with everyone, but especially the very young and the elderly.

He'll sit and watch you talking as if he understands every word. He's particularly fond of classical music and if you have a piano you could find him running up and down the keys, composing quite tuneful (to him!) melodies.

At mealtimes you'll never have to worry about your little goat cat finishing off his food. He'll eat up every last bit and anything that falls off his saucer. Your leftovers will all be eaten up too, but be careful not to give him anything salted, which goes for all cats. Your Capricorn pet also has great endurance. Although he likes stability, he will stoically adapt to every situation, no matter how many upheavals you have in your personal life.

Cool cat

Often Capricorn is lacking in confidence, so he will really appreciate praise and cuddles, even though he's a bit reserved himself and isn't given to open displays of affection. Sometimes he gets upset, but he tends to hide his feelings. He can also be a bit snobby. If he could talk, he would tell you that even though he was a stray way back, or not so way back, he's related to Snowy Kilmarnock Moonbeam 2, winner of Best in the Breed, Persians, at the National Cat Show in 1993. He certainly does look aristocratic – it must be his good bone structure, courtesy of Saturn, his ruling planet. Although he has a sad expression, don't be fooled into thinking that your Capricorn cat has no sense of humour. His is a dry wit, as he displays when he leaves a mouse beneath the portrait you have had painted of him. Your relationship with him will be full of love, admiration and respect – and you will be able to look forward to having your pet around for a long time to come.

Only cat?

The Capricorn cat is quite happy to be the only one, but if another cat is introduced in the family, he will get on well with him, as long as he knows his place and behaves. If you introduce a kitten into your home, he will get all

The ideal owner

This treasure of a cat needs an owner who is kind, practical and consistent, so a **Taurus** or **Virgo** would be ideal, although a Virgo owner would worry because of the Capricorn's doleful expression. There are some signs that get on with their own sign very well and **Capricorn** is one of them. Having the same values, they will rub along very well together. **Scorpio** would also have a special understanding of the Capricorn cat. Both are deep thinkers and enjoy quiet and solitude. They like the finer things of life, such as traditional fine furnishings and good music. Capricorn is unlikely to get on with lively **Gemini**, overpowering **Leo**, nervous **Libra** or madcap **Sagittarius**, while **Pisces** would be too chaotic.

kittenish and play with the newcomer, but will look after him as well, teaching him how to wash, play and fight. He will also mete out discipline with a smart bat of his paw when it is needed!

Food for health

Because these cats live to a ripe old age, they need calcium-rich bones. They usually like meat and fish equally. Small amounts of vitamin E oil and cod liver oil will keep their coats shiny and healthy.

Leaving your Capricorn cat

Your Capricorn will look doleful when you take him to a cattery, but he looks

like this anyway. Actually he will adapt very well. He will be philosophical about your absence and the confined space. After you have gone, he will sit and plan what to do when he gets home. He will also appreciate the routine of a cattery – his meals at set times and the fact that he has a cage to himself. This is an intensely nature-loving cat who will observe the birds and all the wildlife around him with great interest.

AQUARIUS

〰 21 January–19 February

Key characteristics

The Aquarius cat has the key phrase 'I invent.' He is creative and will rarely do the same thing twice. The name Water Carrier is misleading, as Aquarius is in fact an Air sign. The 'water' in this sign's symbol represents knowledge, which Aquarians carry and distribute to those they encounter. These cats are group felines and could bring lots of friends in through the cat flap. They seem absent minded but this is because they are brilliant. They are not particularly emotional on a one-to-one basis but love all creatures, including you!

Interested in everything

When you first take home your little Aquarius, don't think he'll be like all the cats you read about in books, or like those belonging to your friends. He is a one-off and will be as different from the average cat as … well … rabbit is from fish. Although he's very friendly, there remains an air of detachment about him and a faraway look. He loves you, but then he loves nearly everyone and there is such a big world out there to explore. However, he has a good memory and usually remembers where you live, eventually!

Symbol: The Water Carrier

Element: Air

Aquarius rules: Inventions, international charities, groups of cats, friends, societies

Lucky colours: Turquoise, electric blue, mixed colours like tartan – just right for his window seat

Ruling planet: Uranus – springs surprises, revolution, anything ahead of its time

Compatible with: Aries, Gemini, Leo and Sagittarius

Fairly compatible with: Virgo, Libra, Capricorn, Aquarius and Pisces

Not usually compatible with: Taurus, Cancer and Scorpio

Likes
Freedom, space, moving home, visitors, other animals, an easy-going owner

Dislikes
Being picked up and cuddled, restrictions, sitting on laps, confined spaces, an emotional owner

If you are an exclusive person and just want him and no other animals around you, then you are in for a shock. He's very sociable and won't just make friends with the neighbourhood cats, but with all the animals around and your neighbours too. In fact, it won't be just one neighbour who says he's sitting on their sofa, but several will say that he visits them and makes himself at home. He's likely to invite other cats into your home too.

Goes with the flow
He needs other cats and is probably friends with your hamster too.

Aquarius is ruled by the planet Uranus. Surprises, electric shocks, sudden changes, space travel, unusual relationships, inventions and eccentricity come under its influence. Most cats are creatures of habit, but you will find that your Aquarius doesn't sleep in the same place every day and doesn't have regular food times either. One day you will find him sleeping on the highest shelf you have, the next he'll be hidden away in your laundry basket. And he will often skip a meal when he is meditating on life or watching wildlife in the garden. He belongs to the New Age and is ahead of his time.

Surprise package

It's unlikely that your little Aquarius will go into orbit on a space shuttle, but he will spring a few surprises. He is a very bright cat and you could be amazed when he works out how to undo a locked cat flap or open the oven door.

Your Uranus-ruled cat is concerned about the world too, and all the cruelty and injustices in it, especially to animals. He may not be able to vocalize this to you, but he does care, so if you join a few charitable animal organizations, and make some of them international, he will think you are an owner worthy of him.

Like the other Air signs, Aquarius cats are odd emotionally. Although you may think he doesn't really care about you, if you suddenly introduce another cat, or show attention to someone, he could become irrationally jealous and shred your sofa to show his anger. OK, in the past he hasn't minded when you've shown affection to the parrot, your partner or next door's dog, but suddenly the emotional goalposts have changed. Aquarius, being an Air sign, finds emotions difficult to deal

with. But your life will never be dull. How can you ever be bored when you come home from shopping and discover six strange and unusual-looking cats sitting round your fire, all friends of your Aquarius cat!

Unlike your other friends who say their cats don't do very much except eat and sleep, you'll be able to tell stories about your pet's unusual antics, and you'll truly appreciate him.

Only cat?

Whether he's an only cat or one of many, Aquarius won't mind, as even if he is on his own he will soon make friends with the

The ideal owner

Gemini and **Sagittarius** would understand the Aquarius's mental brilliance and need for a wide circle of friends. They would also not be too possessive and would appreciate the need for the Aquarius to have freedom and variety. These signs would be happy to have an open cat flap and wouldn't be too house proud. And his unpredictable habits would stimulate them. Aquarius's opposite sign, **Leo**, might make a good owner as well. The Leo respects Aquarius's individuality. Aries, too, would make a good match. Both have lively minds. But **Taurus** or **Cancer** would be too fixed and family-oriented, and **Scorpio** too possessive and intense.

whole neighbourhood. He also knows how to amuse himself when you are out. And, since he has his own agenda, he may not even notice if you introduce other pets. However, sometimes he is a little quirky and could take a sudden dislike to one of them.

Food for health

Aquarius cats use up a lot of nervous energy and need their B vitamins, which are found in brewer's yeast tablets and liver. (Feed them 1 dessertspoon of liver twice a week maximum). They may like strange foods, such as avocado pears and sweetcorn, but these certainly won't do them any harm.

Leaving your Aquarius cat

You don't have to worry about this cat pining away. He won't mind you jetting off and putting him in a cattery for a week or two. He'll spend the time getting to know the other animals and observing how they behave. Of course, being a bit of an international feline, he would rather come with you, especially if you go somewhere mystical, like Peru, but it may not be convenient to take him to Machu Picchu!

PISCES

♓ 20 February–20 March

Key characteristics

This is the twelfth sign of the zodiac and the Pisces cat's key phrase is 'I dream.' He lives in a world of fantasy and is also a very intuitive creature. He tends to be accident-prone, but usually has only minor mishaps and has more than his share of nine lives. This cat is very adaptable, psychic and sensitive, but is easily hurt. Although difficult to train and very untidy and messy as a kitten, he is playful and his antics will make you forgive his indiscretions. Sometimes he becomes less untidy as he grows older, but he is always loving and makes an excellent family pet.

Water baby

Your Pisces cat will have a faraway look, a round face and big dreamy eyes. It's easy for him to live in a world of fantasy, being born under Neptune, the planet of illusion. He'll sit with you on the sofa and love watching soap operas on TV, and he'll amuse you with his amazing antics. This is a very sensitive, psychic creature and, like the Cancer cat, he is never happier than when he has the whole family around him. He really hates being on his own and needs someone or some other pet around him all the time.

Symbol: Two fish swimming in opposite directions

Element: Water

Pisces rules: Illusion, drugs, the subconscious, dreams, dancing and artistry, imagination, media, the sea

Lucky colours: Silvery grey, misty blue, lilac

Ruling planet: Neptune – the illusionist and creative dreamer

Compatible with: Taurus, Cancer and Aquarius

Fairly compatible with: Virgo, Scorpio, Capricorn, and Pisces

Not usually compatible with: Aries, Gemini, Leo, Libra and Sagittarius

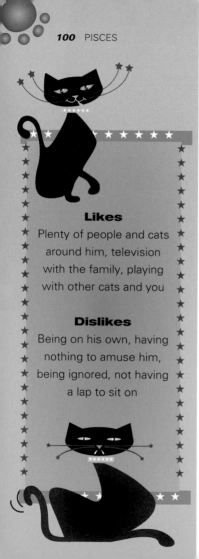

Likes
Plenty of people and cats around him, television with the family, playing with other cats and you

Dislikes
Being on his own, having nothing to amuse him, being ignored, not having a lap to sit on

He'll probably like to watch you in the bath or shower, as he loves water, but as he is accident-prone, watch out he doesn't fall in the bath. In the kitchen, too, you'll find he enjoys playing with the water as it comes out of the tap, perhaps when you are washing vegetables.

Pet insurance vital

It's not just the bathroom and kitchen sink you have to watch out for, as he always seems to be having minor accidents. He could curl up in the washing machine, get locked in closets, shut in garages and burn his paws on your stove. Paw injuries are something he will suffer with particularly, as Pisces rules the paws – from prickles and thorns to crushing injuries caused by human feet. It's a shame you can't fit him with a pair of shoes or boots, but with him they would probably be uncomfortable! The list of possible mishaps is endless and the best thing is to keep a watchful eye on him and remove anything that might be a hazard. Pisces cats have even been known to eat yards of cotton from a reel, with the result that they need an operation to have the cotton removed.

Muddled and moody

The Pisces kitten is also difficult to train, as he is so untidy. Cleanliness isn't his strong point either. To him, behind the sofa or door is just as good a place as the litter tray, but usually as he gets older he gets cleaner, you'll be pleased to hear.

The Pisces cat takes offence easily, and sometimes when you least expect it. Laugh at him once too often when he falls off the sofa when asleep and he could sit with his back to you for hours to show how hurt he is. The Pisces cat also has a temper, which is not always associated in traditional astrology with this sign. If something really annoys him, like a child pulling his tail, he could make his anger felt in no uncertain way with a bat of his paw.

This cat is amazingly adaptable to family changes and upheavals, such as moving house or decorators taking over your home. He just seems to find a nice comfortable place away from all the trouble. He is a very kind-hearted cat and will comfort your family when they are ill, but usually he gets in such scrapes he is the one that is being looked after all the time. He does love to wander, but with his track record for mishaps it's probably best not to let him too far out of your sight. Definitely take out a pet insurance plan for your cat, as you could have to make a great many trips to the vet in his lifetime. But the good news is that he is a true survivor and usually doesn't suffer with major ailments.

Purring passenger

One place he'll probably settle down happily in is your car. He loves travel

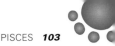

The ideal owner

Fellow Water signs **Scorpio** and **Cancer** are as sensitive as the Pisces cat. They will realize he needs to be loved and amused and share his world of fantasy and fun. And Aquarius cats will share his mad moments. **Taurus** and **Virgo** will also understand this cat in a more practical way. They are both physical and loving, but will put a few gentle boundaries round the chaotic Pisces. These two Earth signs will also be sensitive to the Pisces cat's delicate digestion and will tempt him with a suitable diet. **Leo** owners would be too dominant and **Aries** would rule the poor Pisces without being sensitive to his needs. **Gemini** wouldn't understand his sensitivity, **Libra** is too much on a mental plane and **Sagittarius** would drive Pisces mad with wild exuberance.

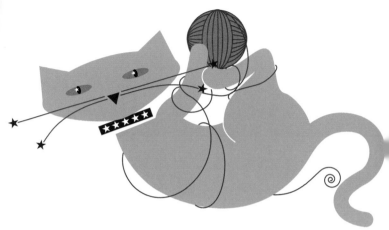

and while he's in a cat carrier, where he can have a good view of everything passing by, he can't come to too much harm. Like the Cancer and Taurus cats, he's a real family pet. When you talk about your family to friends, you'll always mention him as well without even thinking. He is a cat that everyone will take to their hearts.

Only cat?

The Pisces cat is very sociable. He would hate to be left on his own, and introducing another cat can transform his life and make

him really happy, as he loves to play. If you have to leave him on his own, make sure you put some music or a radio on for him. You could even ring him up so he hears your voice on the answerphone.

Food for health

The Pisces cat loves fish, but he does have a delicate digestion and needs a good balanced diet, with not too much at a time. He may get addicted to one type of food, such as tuna, but however much he ignores other foods, a restricted diet like that isn't healthy. Should you reach this impasse, give him something different that is a treat, such as beef or lamb in its own delicious gravy.

Leaving your Pisces cat

Because he hates being on his own, it's kindest to put him in the same pen as one of your other cats, if you have one, when you take him to a cattery. As long as he has plenty of company he should be fine. The Pisces may be a a kitten at heart, but you shouldn't worry as he is amazingly adaptable and when you get him home he'll never stop purring because he will be so pleased to see you again.

At home with your cat

While you jet off abroad for holidays, go out to dinner or go to work, your astrocat will be stuck in the house with, hopefully, access to the garden. And mostly this will comprise his whole world for his entire life. True, if he's allowed, and if he's adventurous, he may wander off and explore the neighbourhood, but with most cats the majority of their days, with perhaps the odd visit to the cattery or vet, consist of living in your home and garden. Therefore, it is important that your house is designed to suit your cat to ensure his ultimate and complete comfort and happiness. He'll be a very contented feline indeed if you can give him the environment of his dreams. So here's the lowdown on the best home and garden for each sign of the zodiac.

The perfect home for the Aries cat

Your energetic, impetuous Aries will appreciate an open-plan home – he's a thoroughly modern cat and hates shut doors. Just leave a small open square in the door for him to come and go, because the most unbreakable cat flap will end up in bits within a couple of days as he charges in and out like a ballistic missile. It might be a bird he's seen, or nothing – he's a cat who has sudden notions. He likes the colour red, and it would be best to furnish your house in tough materials, such as stainless steel. Somehow he never learns to use a scratching post, or retract his claws.

... and his ideal garden

The wilder the better for him – and for you. You don't want your heart broken when, for the hundredth time, he digs up your neat rows of begonias. Give him a play area and a nice, high brick wall that he can caterwaul from and eye up the feline opposition next door.

★★★★★★★★★★★★★★★★★★★★★★★★★★★★

The perfect home for the Taurus cat

You only have to think of four words with the Taurus cat: love, comfort, food and warmth. This cat doesn't need a lot of mental stimulation. He is basic. But he is territorial too, so he'll like the run of the house, plus access to your bedroom. Soft, flower-sprigged fabrics appeal to him and rustic, cottage or farmhouse rooms will suit him. He doesn't mind a bit of chaos – he's not exactly tidy himself. He's a real country-loving cat, but don't worry if you can't live in the country, as long as he has his creature comforts, he'll be fine.

... and his ideal garden

He's a sensuous beast, so he'll love scented flowers; for example: roses, lily of the valley and, of course, catmint. To stop him nibbling it to the root, try growing some in a hanging basket. He likes to be secure too, so a high fence will allow him to sunbathe in peace.

The perfect home for the Gemini cat

The Gemini cat likes to be amused, and this lively, Mercury-ruled feline will enjoy a modern, airy house with lots going on, heaps of people and cats and all the latest gadgets, like electronic flea zappers and remote-controlled toy mice. As this cat is so vocal, he will like the sound of the stereo, radio or television to add noise and interest. The mind-stimulating colour yellow is his favourite, so add this to your decor.

... and his ideal garden

Something modern and sophisticated, perhaps with lots of decking, wind chimes and carefully designed play areas will suit him. He doesn't mind if there isn't too much greenery, as long as there's enough foliage to prowl in. Playing and being curious about the neighbours are his main joys. He will also enjoy discovering local haunts. Low fences will suit him, enabling him to see what's going on next door and wander around the other gardens. This cat needs an identity tag on his collar, as he could get lost through curiosity.

★★★★★★★★★★★★★★★★★★★★★★★★★★★★★★★★★★

The perfect home for the Cancer cat

Your Cancer cat needs a real family home with lots of old, comfy cushions and a traditional look. The kitchen will definitely be his favourite room, not only because of the food but also because the family congregates there. He likes to feel enclosed, so a round cat basket with a soft interior will give him a secure place to sniff the cooking and view your kitchen table. He will definitely want to stay with you at night too, and will probably sleep on one of the children's beds. He won't be too happy about other cats coming into the home, so a lockable cat flap is ideal for him. Soft shades of sea green, pale moonlight blue and pearly white are his favourite colours.

... and his ideal garden

Although he likes to wander, he can also feel insecure, so he will appreciate high walls around your garden. Being a water sign, he will enjoy a water feature, even if it is just a small fountain. He loves the sea, so you could have a nautical theme somewhere, whether it is shells or an anchor.

★★★★★★★★★★★★★★★★★★★★★★★★★★★★★★

The perfect home for the Leo cat

Think luxury when you adapt your home for your regal Leo puss – sunny rooms with plenty of gold, yellow and orange. He likes everything to be on the large side, from his feeding bowl and meals, to his bed and cat carrier. A castle would suit him, of course, but if you can't stretch to that, you could paint a coat of arms or crown on his carrier. He loves warmth, so let him have a south-facing room and a fire to stretch out in front of in winter.

... and his ideal garden

The regal theme can be continued in the garden with lion statuary and a sundial, as the Sun is his ruling planet. A small sunbed, modelled on yours, will make him feel special. He likes everything on a grand scale and golden flowers such as sunflowers, marigolds and nasturtiums will cheer him. And, of course, ideally the garden should face south to get the benefit of all the fine weather.

★★★★★★★★★★★★★★★★★★★★★★★★★★★★★★

The perfect home for the Virgo cat

Think of a hospital and you can't go far wrong. Your Virgo likes things neat, simple and spanking clean. Fussy ornaments are out, and you can serve his food in a simple stainless-steel bowl or plain white saucer. White is a soothing colour for Virgo – with white they know if things are clean or not. Green, the colour of nature, is also perfect for cushions, curtains and cat beds.

... and his ideal garden

A simple green lawn with neat flowerbeds and white flowers gives Virgo the peace and tranquillity he craves. He doesn't like anything too fussy, but he will appreciate plenty of greenery and beautiful flowers. He also loves to listen to the sound of the wind in the trees and will watch everything going on in the garden for hours, whether it's the shadows of plants and birds or whatever's happening in your neighbour's garden. He is a little nosy.

The perfect home for the Libra cat

This cat will appreciate space and minimalism, but perhaps with a gentle traditional feel. He will like the rooms to be light and sunny, furnished in pastels of blue, pink or lemon and with comfortable, soft cushions to relax on, preferably ones that tone nicely with the shade of his fur. He appreciates art, beauty and classical music, although he does like some modern compositions as well.

... and his ideal garden

The Libra cat would enjoy one of the modern Zen gardens, with a small temple, a peaceful water feature and some gentle wind chimes. Like the Pisces cat, he loves pastel, Monet-type colours with blurred edges to the borders and petal-strewn paths. He likes the garden to be a haven where he can meditate and recharge his batteries. But as he is also a very sociable cat at times and enjoys eating al fresco, a small patio with relaxing garden chairs will be perfect for you and him to entertain your respective friends.

★★★★★★★★★★★★★★★★★★★★★★★★★★★★★★

The perfect home for the Scorpio cat

This is a cat who craves dark and mysterious places to hide away in. He will love an attic that he can retreat to when the rest of the house is too busy or you have visitors. On the whole, he likes dark colours, including wine, black and grey. He particularly likes cellars, not just because there could be the odd mouse down there, but because of the whole ambience of being underground, including the musty smell.

... and his ideal garden

Gothic towers and arches with plenty of secret arbours will suit the Scorpio. Dark, wine-coloured flowers and scarlet, sleepy poppies will appeal to him and, as he is a Water sign, a water feature would soothe him, preferably with still water. Scorpio's element is still, deep water, and having an unfathomable personality, it would suit him perfectly.

★★★★★★★★★★★★★★★★★★★★★★★★★★★★★★

The perfect home for the Sagittarius cat

This independent cat needs plenty of freedom and space. Open plan suits him perfectly. He is very much an outdoor hunter, so unless it's bitterly cold, he won't be spending much time inside anyway. But he is incredibly clumsy, so he needs a home where everything is unbreakable. Ornaments should be locked away and forget about flowers in vases unless you keep them in a room he can't get into. His muddy paws will leave dirty marks everywhere he goes, so make sure surfaces can be wiped clean.

... and his ideal garden

Wild and wonderful will suit him, with indigenous shrubs and trees, long grasses and weeds. If this kind of natural look doesn't appeal, you could give him an overgrown area at the end of the garden instead. Such a place will also have the added bonus of attracting bees and butterflies to your garden.

★★★★★★★★★★★★★★★★★★★★★★★★★★★★★★★★★★★★★

The perfect home for the Capricorn cat

Capricorn prefers a neat, orderly home, with everything always in the same place and meals served on time. He veers to the traditional in furnishings, favouring formal, antique furniture upholstered in brown, black, garnet and natural colours. And he'll be able to adapt to living almost anywhere, being frugal and accommodating by nature. He can live in a flat probably better than any other sign, but he does like plenty of things to climb up and usually he prefers his cushions and bed on the firm side. Many Capricorn cats favour a chilly atmosphere to a warm one, being a cool character and ruled by the sombre planet Saturn.

... and his ideal garden

The grounds of grand, aristocratic homes would suit this cat, with formal arrangements, neat box hedges, geometric flowerbeds, lead containers and topiary. He will love to sun himself on the elegant sweep of the stone steps. Add tall cedar and beech trees to climb and he'll be in his element.

The perfect home for the Aquarius cat

Think New Age with this creature. His ruling planet, Uranus, also rules space travel, so give him lots of futuristic furniture and loads of space, with pale colours offset by myriad colourful stripes or tartans and electric blues and silvers. As well as needing personal space, Aquarius wants lots of room for the friends he brings back through the cat flap.

... and his ideal garden

Everything that is modern or eccentric will suit the Aquarius, giving him somewhere to meditate on life and entertain his various friends. Like the Libra cat, he will enjoy a Japanese or Zen garden, as he loves anything unusual or exotic. He likes to feel that he is a truly international creature. He is very *animalitarian* (the equivalent of humanitarian!) and will respect other life forms, such as butterflies, bees, mice and even you.

★★★★★★★★★★★★★★★★★★★★★★★★★★★★★★★★

The perfect home for the Pisces cat

Relax – you don't need to be houseproud to please a Pisces. This cat is so playful he loves a bit of a shambles – balls of wool strewn across the floor and untidy beds. He's fascinated by water, so he'll pad around the bathroom or perch himself on the kitchen sink. Ruled by the planet Neptune, which also rules television and dancing, he'll love to sit himself down with the family and watch ballet or wildlife programmes on TV. Gossamer colours, such as silvers, misty blues and greys, make him feel at home. He is also quite artistic – a Monet painting will please, especially if it contains a few fish.

... and his ideal garden

Curved and undulating flowerbeds that spill over with an abundance of untidy roses, larkspur and love-in-a-mist will be the ideal place for your Pisces cat to stretch out and daydream. A small fountain would also delight him, as would a willow tree or a weeping cherry.

Future trends

What lies in the future for our cats? New legislation is being introduced to protect pets, which can only be a good thing. Gandhi once said, 'You can judge a nation by the way it treats its animals.' So how do we, in the West, measure up?

Many of us spend small fortunes on our pets while, sadly, the same species can still be used in legal experiments to test household products and for medical science. It would seem that in our so-called civilized society there is still a lot of hypocrisy.

But astrology has a message for the future. The outer planets, Pluto and Neptune, now in the compassionate signs of Sagittarius and Aquarius for several years to come, herald a more caring and environmentally aware age. Already we are demanding purer, organic food for ourselves, but many of us don't extend this ethos to our pets. Let's hope that in this new age we will treat our pets better. Then, we can truly call ourselves a civilized society – one of which Gandhi would have been proud.

Index

About the author

Julia Harris is an astrologer, poet and journalist, and writes Astrocats for Britain's bestselling cat magazine, *Your Cat.* Her work has appeared in *The Lady* and *Prediction Annual,* and her poetry has been reviewed in the *Times Literary Supplement.*

Acknowledgements

Executive Editor: Trevor Davies
Managing Editor: Clare Churly
Executive Art Editor: Joanna
        MacGregor
Designer: Elizabeth Healey
Illustrations: Line and Line
Senior Production Controller:
        Jo Sim